MW01295361

Paths that Intertwine

I first met Roberto (Bob) Prinselaar the 31st of October 1990 while doing a Social Work student placement at the Vet Center in Las Vegas, Nevada. (I went on to be a readjustment Counselor there until July 1992). I was the person processing new intakes that day. Something established an immediate bond between us, perhaps it was the fact that we had some common memories of the song "China Night" which is well known to those who had been in the "Land of the Frozen Chosen" during the 1950's.

After playing a copy of that song, Bob brought a collection of poems into the Vet Center, without order, all in his hand writing. I asked if I might make copies, little did I realize then that any copies of this collection would be published.

While typing. I began to feel the anger, anguish, futility and mistrust that had been put on paper by this quiet man. As I reread, typed and retyped, a strange feeling settled over me, maybe, just maybe there might really be something to the statement made by Bob "I wake up in the morning and there on my desk will be a poem in my handwriting, but I cannot remember writing it!" I realize now that our paths were destined to intertwine, thus insuring these poems would not be lost or forgotten, but brought to other Veterans, so that they might not agonize as Bob has.

One of the poems kept flashing into my mind, "Pieces of Myself", continued to bother me in an unexplainable way until I returned from a trip in 1990 to the wall. Wile standing at the "*Wall*" the first night we were in D.C., a cold and rainy November night, searching for my cousin's name, *Mark Stoltenburg*; the thought came to me that the rain we were experiencing was the tears of those who had gone before for those of us left behind and who are still suffering. Mark was a Marine "Semper Fi" and I was Air Force and in "the Nam" at the same time in 1966; I returned, Mark did not!

Upon returning to the Vet Center I was once again bothered by the poem "*Pieces of Myself*". I sat at my desk and spotted a piece of blank Vet Center stationary lying there. The last line of the poem came to me "*Or am I lost without the key*", looking at the logo and seeing part of a skeleton key that unlocks old closets or attics, I then modified the Vet Center Logo into the shape of a key. I decided if you have a key you must have something to unlock. That something turned out to be the mental prison that veterans find themselves in. I simply asked veterans to read "*Pieces of Myself*" and a "*Letter to a Veteran*". This combination was Bob's and my way of showing each Veteran that he/she is not alone!

Thank you for bringing Bob into my life, who ever **you** are!

Chad Avery, LSW

Tears of Ink

Tears of Ink

LCDR Roberto J. Prinselaar
U.S. Coast Guard (Ret)

iUniverse, Inc.

New York Lincoln Shanghai

Tears of Ink

Copyright © 2007 by Roberto J. Prinselaar

All rights reserved. No part of this book may be used or reproduced by any means, graphic, electronic, or mechanical, including photocopying, recording, taping or by any information storage retrieval system without the written permission of the publisher except in the case of brief quotations embodied in critical articles and reviews.

iUniverse books may be ordered through booksellers or by contacting:

iUniverse
2021 Pine Lake Road, Suite 100
Lincoln, NE 68512
www.iuniverse.com
1-800-Authors (1-800-288-4677)

Because of the dynamic nature of the Internet, any Web addresses or links contained in this book may have changed since publication and may no longer be valid.

The views expressed in this work are solely those of the author and do not necessarily reflect the views of the publisher, and the publisher hereby disclaims any responsibility for them.

Permission to use any of the poems contained in this book is hereby granted, with the following proviso, the author must be given credit at each time of use, and they may not be used for monetary gain.

ISBN: 978-0-595-46230-8 (pbk)
ISBN: 978-0-595-90531-7 (ebk)

Printed in the United States of America

To all of the veterans past and present
To all of those who have seen the elephant
To all of those we left behind
To the Vet Centers who strive to help
To all who have stood by us in our need

"You know the real meaning of peace only
if you have been through the war."

—Kosovar

"Only the dead have seen the end of war."

—Plato

6-11-'09

To MY GOOD
FRIEND CARL ALLEN
U.S.C.G.

FROM OLD "SMITTY"
U.S.S. CALIFORNIA BB 44
U.S.N.

THE DAY THAT WILL
"LIVE IN INFAMY."

DEC. 7- 1941

Contents

Acknowledgements

I thank all of the veterans from all the services, but most of all I thank the Vet Centers for making me aware that there could be a way to alleviate the problems I had, a result of my military experiences. I met others much like me, and was able to reignite a feeling of camaraderie, that was lacking in my civilian existence. Although my counselor at the center tried very hard to get me to talk about my past, I found that the simple act of putting my thoughts on paper helped me the most. The fact that I was able to use poems to express my feelings, I fully consider a gift from a higher source, and I am very thankful.

I also want to thank everyone who knew me, and put up with me. It must have been hard at times, since I was not always easy to get along with. I sincerely hope that by reading what I have written I will be more fully understood, and that my writings will help another veteran to more fully understand his/her own feelings.

Chad Avery, a fellow veteran, and a counselor at the Las Vegas, Nevada, Vet Center, when we first met, was the first to recognize the value of my poems, and suggest publishing them to benefit veterans from all wars.

My wife, Arlene, has been a great source of love and inspiration, and is, to a great degree, responsible for my publishing these poems, at this time.

Tears Of Ink

My tears of ink flow down my pen
A torrent of what's inside of me
My feelings in a tale
The words all come from deep within
Old memories just come tumbling out
As I pull aside the veil
Some memories darker than the ink
And I fight to keep them down
My hand grips hard the pen
Why am I cursed with all my thoughts
Of things that happened long ago
And of men I knew back then
So now I write to ease the pain
And I cry inside to form the ink
And let it flow to write
But ink will never be the same
And I will never find my peace
Till real tears blur my sight

The Bullet

The bullet was fired, not into space but into time
Instead of lead and brass, the bullet was made up of many things
Of pain, and gut wrenching grief
Of hatred and rage so fierce, it glowed
Of lost friends and buddies and guys you barely knew
Of fear so bad you made your own midnight movies
But hid so well
But mostly of memories which were unwanted
And smells that came from hell

When the bullet was fired it was outgoing and therefore good
But because it went into time it changed over the years
And even though it was mostly forgotten
It was still in flight, and as a comet it turned
Even though misted by time
It became incoming with no place to hide

The bullet came and pierced my soul
I had bunkered my life, my defenses were strong
So I thought
Then the layers of shell all fell away, and I was caught naked
And it started again
All the crap in the bullet was with me again
And now
I'm living and dying
All over again

I'm O.K.

I'll admit I'm slightly troubled
And there are times I'm downright sad
When I think back on things that happened
And some of those were really bad
But I'm O.K., I tell you truly
I'm alive, and that's a lot
I'm better off than some old buddies
Yeah I'm alive, and they are not
There are times I dream about them
But mostly now, I only sleep
I'm telling you I'm doing fine now
Why should I think 'bout things so deep
I never cry, cause that's not manly
It's not the way that I was taught
And what the hell, it's all behind me
I've put aside just why we fought
I can't remember all the reasons
There had to be some, I suppose
I do remember, for God and country
But it was more than only those
I lost some friends, for lofty reasons
And now they are forever gone
But I'm O.K., yeah I'm still living
But sometimes God, I'm so alone

Poems

I'm not a fancy poet
I just write what's in my heart
I just write it like I feel it
And that sets me apart
I don't try to be a real dandy
And I don't turn a fancy phrase
You can tell just what I'm saying
Just by looking at my face
Cause I feel the things I'm writing
And they sometimes bring a tear
When I write about long lost buddies
Wartime memories bring them near
Yeah, my poems sure ain't fancy
And my grammar took a rest
But does all that really matter
When I write about the best
Of all the guys who still remember
Just a few of us can write
And we try to bring some daylight
To this everlasting night
Most of us were just enlisted
And we didn't have much couth
But if you listen very closely
It's from us you'll hear the truth
You won't hear about no glory
Or about the medals we have won
But you might hear about our buddies
How we're glad the war is done
It don't matter where we fought
Or which war that had to be

All the guys know what I'm saying
That's what matters most to me
So I think I'll just keep writing
Listen close to what I say
Maybe then you'll know what war's like
And hope to God it stays away

Anniversaries

I think of anniversaries
Of the things that brought me pain
Of all the things that happened then
That drove me near insane
I've kept those anniversaries
Never knowing that I did
But they keep coming back each year
No matter how I hid
We all have anniversaries
Of good things and of bad
And there are some we celebrate
That damn near drive us mad
A friend of mine would celebrate
For guys who were now dead
And then one day he joined them all
With a bullet in his head
Another friend would think way back
And his tears would be a flood
So one fine day he cut his wrists
And we found him in his blood
I don't know why we celebrate
Those things of long ago
We try to leave them in the past
But try won't make it so
The anniversaries just keep slipping in
No matter what we do
I guess we'll have them till we die
Until our lives are through
And most of us will struggle on
Not knowing when or why

We just keep having special days
When we sit down to cry
I guess someday I'll know the truth
When my dream comes to take
And lets me see it all the way
When I know that I'm awake

A Hill

Have you ever tried to climb a hill

And found it was too steep

Have you ever had some dreams so bad

You were afraid to go to sleep

And while awake, have you ever thought

That some things don't seem real

So you pinch yourself, a little hurt

But that's not the pain you feel

Cause inside you have a lasting pain

That will never go away

And your memories are reminders

That the pain is here to stay

To tell someone is so very hard

Of the things that you've been through

So you walk through life a wounded man

And all your friends get wounded too

Combat

Roaring noises

Screaming voices

Metal flying

There and here

Eyes are burning

Guts are churning

Men are fighting

Full of fear

Guns are smoking

Lungs are choking

Through it all

Godawful smell

I hear crying

Men are dying

I'm alive

But I'm in hell

Medals

Don't envy a man his medals
All those ribbons on his chest
He did not try to get them
They're not there at his request
They were earned in stinking hell holes
Where no man would like to go
Or in cold and wintry places
Where there's only ice and snow
He did not know he earned them
Till they were awarded at parade
And they were bright when he first got them
But in time the colors fade
He was told he had to wear them
And to wear them all with pride
But when the memories come to haunt him
Those same medals make him hide
Cause those medals will not bring back
All those guys he left behind
And he would trade them all forever
For a little peace of mind
So don't envy a man his medals
You don't want to take his place
Thinking back to long gone battles
And meeting dead friends face to face

Ghost

He looked at me
And never saw
I spoke to him
He never heard
He was a boy
But now a man
He tried to speak
But not a word
Black holes for eyes
Sunk in his head
A thousand yards
His eyes did stare
He'd made it through
A yesterday
And lived with pain
So hard to bear
From day to day
With all hope gone
Another day
He'd have to try
He must have known
He must have felt
He stared at fate
Today he'd die

Head Pain

The pain feels like exploding fire
As the knife slides through to the bone
My head hurts like this often now
Oh my God I'm so alone
The doctor says "There's nothing wrong"
I am just "A bit too tense"
Relax, he says, it's good for you
Now that's just common sense
But lately that's so hard to do
When I know the knife will come
And I hope the pain won't hurt so bad
If I drink a little rum
Or maybe just a couple of beers
I've always like that stuff
I remember beer eased all my pain
When I was young and times were rough
All my friends and I would gather then
And we would drink to ease our pain
It was better to get roaring drunk
Than to think and go insane
They're all gone now, I'm alone
With this fire in my head
And I can blame it on myself now
For the things I've never said
The pain is real, it's not a joke
And I don't know what to do
For the knife just keeps on coming
Piercing my head through and through

Independence Day

Independence Day, or fourth of July
What is the name to me
Independence Day, is a special day
With lots of meaning for me

The fourth of July is another thing
It is just another day
While the fourth of July may come and go
Our Independence is here to stay

Our Independence was won, by iron willed men
Who had nothing special to gain
They fought for their freedom, and that of their sons
They fought through hardship and pain

Valley Forge was a winter they had to endure
And many men died of the cold
But the ones that survived were harder than steel
An Army of the brave and bold

Cornwallis at Yorktown finally surrendered
And our Army could call itself free
So I'll never forget, our Independence
And those men who got it for me

More than 200 years, we're still independent
And more men have died for the cause
Freedom is paid for, it never was free
Each man is a terrible loss

So I look at my flag with all of it's stars
And the 13 stripes to the side
I stand at attention and snap a salute
And I'm filled with a wonderful pride

Me

For years and years I really did
Keep all my bad thoughts safely hid
Those bad-assed memories tucked away
If someone asked, I wouldn't say
A real tough bastard, that was me
no one could touch me can't you see
The past was past and buried deep
And only sometimes I couldn't sleep
The first years were hard, a real bitch
Like I was doing another hitch
I drank a lot and went through hell
███████████████████████████████

All this went on ten years or so
I wasn't dead, so more to go
I saw a doctor once, a shrink
A real know nothing civvie dink
I felt forgotten and alone
There just was no one in my zone
That's when I built my private wall
██████████████████████████████

I could face the world with no fear
I kept a pistol always near
Now that was one thing I could trust
Some firepower, a real must
I really straightened up my life
With lots of help from my dear wife
I told her nothing, to be sure
Why take the chance without the cure
And then one day I saw the wall
Upon my life it cast a pall

But another vet said "Welcome Back"
My solid wall began to crack
It was then, I dared to cry
My prior years were just a lie
I had to face my times in hell
Another vet, someone to tell
I'm going to climb this goddamn hill
It may be steep and I may fall
But in the end, I'll tell it all

Memorials

There are memorials to just about every goddamn war the good
Old U.S. of A. ever fought
There are even memorials to certain events which occurred
During those years
What really pisses me off
What about all that shit that happened between wars
What about all those poor forgotten and unnamed sons of bitches
Who sweated, bled, and died
In places no one will ever hear or read about
Threatened with courts martial if they talked
Looked upon as sub human because of what they were capable of
and did
Torn apart inside by the things seen and done
And never, not ever, allowed to talk to no one
Goddamn the pain
Goddamn the memories
Goddamn the sons of bitches who allowed it to happen
But most of all—goddamn me
Thanks for allowing me to be at places which did rate mention
Thanks for allowing me to attend reunions where I can talk
Thanks for allowing me to live
But most of all thanks for easing my dreams
Now I look at memorials and see faces
The only names I knew were nicknames
Not what they put on memorials
Now they are a lost legion
Never to be found
Memorials

Mists Of Time

The mists of time surround me
Deep shadows dark within
I grope for unseen answers
A contest I must win
The years have grown upon me
They slide by like the mist
Within those years so many names
Those blank spots on the list
I know I used to know them
At least I knew their name
Why are they now forgotten men
The ghosts that bring me shame
For I'm alive and they are not
Why did they have to go
Cause I was there, And I'm still here
But why? I just don't know
I still look for the answers
I've looked with all my might
But the dark mist still surrounds me
and fills my soul with fright
Why do their ghosts still haunt me
Why can't they let me be
Why won't they lift the mist of time
And let my soul be free

Of Guns And Friends

I lie wrapped in folds of armor plate
Within my home as gray as slate
I'm far away from land and shore
In peaceful sleep on a man of war
Come light of day and morning sun
I'll check the functions of my gun
I'll check the point, and then the train
And then I'll check it all again
For that's the gun that let's me sleep
And keeps me from a grave so deep
I'm now asleep, my mind at peace
But will my battles never cease?
The years have gone, the gun is rust
So many friends are now just dust
But they are never far from me
Although some sleep beneath the sea
For them no songs are ever sung
But they will be forever young
Friends and relations shed their tears
Forgotten now these many years
But some of us remember still
Remember them, and always will
I ask them now for my release
Or will my battles never cease

Parts Of Us

I talked to another vet today
About some of the guys we knew
And about some problems we still have
Because part of us died there too
It's oh so hard to talk today
About things from long ago
About things that gave us nightmares
For our terror midnight show
There were guys who lost their lives
And then some who took their own
They did a number on us all
And they shook us to the bone
What they did was not uncommon
We've all thought it now and then
But we drew strength from those around us
All those other fighting men
But parts of us died with those others
And we will never be the same
And we will always have one question
Can we forgive the ones to blame

Running (Don't Help)

I tried to run so far away
So I could love and live and play
But running only brought me fear
So far away from things so dear

A foreign land I chose to dwell
No one to know, no one to tell
A place where I could bury me
A stranger, but a stranger free

I thought my life would all be fun
But from the past I couldn't run
I searched for others of my kind
And there were some could read my mind

And I met some who fought there too
So many years and now so few
A foreign flag they proudly hailed
But as for me, I knew I'd failed

My own fair country calls me back
There are my roots, the friends I lack
I've often felt the urge to run
But I'm coming home, the race is done

Punchbowl, Honolulu, Hawaii

Veterans all, they lie sleeping in the punchbowl of Oahu
They died in places with names strange and alien,
    which became household words to most Americans
Guadalcanal, Tarawa, Iwo Jima, Leyte and then Okinawa
God, how many, the toll was a terrible thing
Then a short pause, for everyone to take a breath
Then came Pusan, Inchon, Seoul, the Yalu, and the frozen Chosin
In between all of these places were a thousand valleys and
    ridges where men struggled, bled, and died, over and over again
More names were added to the list in a place called Viet Nam
And thousands more joined all of those other sleeping vets
The punchbowl is strangely quiet now. Few come to visit
It doesn't even look the same anymore
The above ground markers, all white, in their endless rows,
    all gone.
Why?
Now flat plates cover each grave, barely seen
Now lawnmowers can mow without being interfered with
Tourists can come without being shocked at the number of those silent
    graves.
What is not seen can easily be forgotten
Some of us go, and cry with remembrance
Fellow veterans, men who were there
Oh God, how it all still hurts
After all these years
And then to go to the punchbowl, and see what has been done
The terrible truth seems to be
Monuments are only temporary
Remembrance for some is forever
And the grass needs to be mowed

Sometimes

Sometimes

The pain is great
And I hurt like hell

Sometimes

The sadness comes
And the world around me darkens

Sometimes

I need to be alone
And I search for lonely places

Sometimes

I hear others tell
And I am chilled with icy cold

Sometimes

My memories come back
And I could cry, like a child

Sometimes

I think of death
And all the peace that it would bring
but only

Sometimes

Memorial Day

Politicians talk and tell their lies
When they tell us of the who's and why's
They stay behind to have the say
To who will fight and who will stay
Then there are ones who stand to gain
A real nice war without the pain
For every war they make the tools
Then put them in the hands of fools
Yes fools are we who go to fight
Cause fooled are we who think its right
Politicians say it's for our land
For God and country, ain't that grand
They wave the flag in all its glory
But waving flags ain't all the story
The flags we'll see in later years
Will make us think and bring the tears
Where did we go, what did we do
What of our friends whose lives are through
The war we fought will never leave
The memories stay to make us grieve
The war goes on, an endless lane
And we are filled with endless pain
Memorial Day, a day to cry
While politicians smile, and tell a lie

Memorial Day Flags

My flag, my flag, my beautiful flag

I see you everywhere

What do you mean, to all of us

And do we really care

When you pass by at the head of marching men

How many really look

And realize that we're free, we have our land

And wonder what it took

Just witness all the markers, row on endless row

And know these were our sons

They were the ones who fought our wars

And faced the enemy guns

And now they're gone, but on this day

There's a flag above their grave

My flag, your flag, our beautiful flag

Remind us what they gave

Of Eyes That Died

Watch people live
Watch people die
Learn not to care
Learn not to cry
Make many friends
Then watch them go
But thinking friends
Don't make it so
I go to war
I learn the score
From what I saw
My heart is tore
I looked at faces
Young and old
Their eyes had died
The truth be told
And now I dream
Of all those eyes
And now I read
Official lies
But I was told
I could not tell
So I must wait
Till I'm in hell
But until then
I'll be alright
I've learned to live
By dark of night

Ode To A Veteran's Wife

So much pain
And so much sorrow
So many days
Of tear filled eyes
You were there
When life seemed empty
When dark clouds
Filled my rainy skies
You held me close
When I woke sweating
From my nightmares
Filled with cries
I don't know how
You stayed there with me
When I would curse
And tell you lies
Through all the hurt
You are still with me
And if I've won
You are my prize

Medal Of Honor

I met a true hero today
A man who was weathered and old
His face bore the scars
Of the far off fought wars
And all things we never were told

He wore just one medal
It was faded and blue
With little white stars
Round his neck neath the scars
And it showed he was faithful and true

I walked up to that man
And I stood ramrod straight
And like a young boot
I snapped a salute
While I thought of what gave him his fate

I know men like this
I'll meet seldom and few
And I can't help but stare
Cause they're priceless and rare
Those heroes wearing medals of blue

My Pistol

The barrel of my pistol
Feels cold against my head
Why don't I squeeze the trigger
Let loose the final lead
At times I feel such sorrow
My thoughts deep in the past
That's when I think of going
And give me peace at last
But I remember others
Who did that very thing
To leave us with our nightmares
To hear the death knell ring
My memories are too vivid
Of things I cannot tell
Of red things twisted in my mind
Of things that smell of hell
But I won't find my salvation
From the barrel of my gun
I must fight on forever
For I am Odin's son

Misery

Thousands die in every war

But who in hell is keeping score

Statistics tell of battles won

But those were men, somebody's son

No care for medals on his chest

They don't matter, he's now at rest

And all the friends he's ever met

Swear up and down they won't forget

But time works strange things in us all

He wasn't there, he didn't fall

A wall is built, their names all there

We heal ourselves and show we care

We think of all the ones we've lost

And we're the ones who know the cost

The war we fought to keep men free

And all it brought—was misery

Paths

The paths we follow through our lives
Are never very clear
We stumble in the fog of life
And try to hide our fear
We search for everlasting friends
Those ones amongst the few
To find ourselves still all alone
For they are searching too
We grasp adventure like a straw
To feel alive and well
To know you're riding on the edge
And feel the heat of hell
Oh God, I need the feel of love
A family of my own
I have my wife, thank God for her
But damn, I'm so alone
It's better yet to ride the edge
And hope the fall is fast
To end this struggle in the dark
And end my painful past
I can't end now, no matter how
I can't desert my wife
She game me reasons to fight on
I can't give up my life

Pieces Of Myself

Pieces of myself fall on the page

I'm trapped within my inner cage

The bars are here, I cannot run

I'm prevented by the things I've done

Will someone help and understand

And help me with a friendly hand

Though silence is my armor plate

I must have help, fore it's too late

It's hard, for I'm behind these bars

Made by myself from ancient scars

But if I talk will I be free

Or am I lost without the *key*

Politics

I saw my Congressman today
He was busy with a welfare case
"Get out of here you beat up vet"
I just don't want to see your face
You come in here, all sad and blue
Why can't you see, you bother us
So you got shot, or sprayed, or hurt
You're nothing but a lot of fuss
Yes, I remember my campaign
But promises don't mean a thing
I don't see money in your hand
And money's what my good friends bring
You fought the wars way over there
For God and Country's what you said
Now I was smart, I got deferred
I wasn't "crazy in the head"
I left confused and sorry too
Back to the street to walk and roam
What happened to the land I love?
What happened to my "Welcome Home"?????

My Mind

My mind expands

Flows outward from my inner self

Through empty valleys

To a distant hill

I search for life

Through lonely hollows of my soul

And feel the wind

The empty void within me fill

From high above

My view unending through the mist of time

I float and feel

The magnet of my ancient past

I see them buried

In blood rich soil of battle grounds

They talk to me

And tell me to find peace at last

Red

Oh Red
Why did you do it
Why didn't you
Think of us
We were
Your closest buddies
Why didn't you
Think of us
I know
Three of your best friends
Are gone
But it wasn't
Cause of you
They died
And left you living
But there was nothing
You could do
We'd all gone
Through hell together
But we made it
Most of us
So Red
Why did you do it
Why didn't you
Think of us
I wish I could forgive you

Sadness Oh Sadness

Sadness oh sadness
Why don't you leave me
Why can't my past
Just set me free
I'm happy, I'm happy
Oh please can't you see
So sadness oh sadness
Why don't you leave me

You hide in dark corners
Way back in my mind
I walk in bright sunlight
But shadows I find
My life is now happy
So try to be kind
So sadness oh sadness
Please leave my mind

I'm growing old now
I've so much in my past
In roles of much sadness
I've often been cast
My life is now happy
I hope it will last
So sadness oh sadness
Please stay in the past

Questions?

Oh warrior with your head held high
Why are you gazing at the sky?

Why did you fight, Why did you strive?
Or did you think, "Just stay alive"

No matter now for you are here
Alive and healthy it would appear

You have no scars, Your body's whole
What of your mind, What of your soul?

Can you relive the things you've done?
Can you feel safe without a gun?

Can you live fearless off the track?
Without a hard wall at your back?

Do you think drink will hide the hurt?
Do you still jump and hit the dirt?

Did you promise to tell all that you hide?
And then you failed, And then you lied

If this is true, Your life's a mess
You must find help, Call it confess

Have guts have balls, And tell it true
It really helps, I'm telling you

Oh yes it hurts, It isn't fun
But you'll feel better when it's done

Senses

I close my eyes
And I can see
Those awful sights
Of memory
There is no sound
But I can hear
The sounds of battle
Drawing near
I do not touch
And yet I feel
The searing heat
Of burning steel
And no one listens
when I talk
And no one sees
My lonely walk
For I'm alone
So very much
And what I need
Is a friendly touch

The Last Son

An exploding shell
In a manmade hell
And I was fixed for life
No little feet
No small heartbeat
No children with my wife
No child is born
With guts so torn
My memento from a gun
Years come and go
And this I know
I'll never have a son
I'm looking back
On my life's track
I only have my past
My father's son
The only one
And now I'll be the last

The Fury

The fury came
He raised his arm
His fist grasped rock within
He struck so swift
He killed his foe
He was the first to sin
So many years
Have come and gone
The weapons are all new
Instead of killing
Just one man
One hundred are just a few
The first one killed
We know not why
But kill he did we know
He was the first
A fighting man
The first to strike a blow
Throughout the years
How much has changed
We still strike out in fear
We now know why
Or so we say
To guard all we hold dear
We now wage war
Against our foe
Whole nations we can kill
Why don't we ask
When will it end?
When will we have our fill?

Just look our foes
Straight in the eye
And hope you both will live
Present your gift
Just make it life
It's the best that you can give

The Sailor

I have sailed the mighty oceans
Weathered many a raging storm
I have seen so many places
Not a one of them my home
I have served on ships of battle
Helped to feed the cannons roar
Watched the fallen slide forever
Through the sea to ocean floor
I've seen the red of flowing lava
I've seen the ice break on our bow
I've seen fakirs do their magic
To this day I don't know how
I have been in Buddhist Temples
Saw old tribesmen paint their face
Saw more war in parts of Asia
I was glad to leave that place
I've shook with fever from malaria
I've also frozen in the night
When an ice floe broke our mooring
And I yearned for morning light
In bars from here to other places
I've been drunk, and laughed, and fought
Yes, I've truly been a sailor
And it's the world that I've been taught

The Guys I Served With

Who were the guys surrounding me
Everyone an individual and separate entity

The black and brown and white were here
They came from states both far and near

We ate and slept and worked and fought
But always as a team like we were taught

Cause from the team came strength and might
As a team we could win most any fight

Each man was like family, Each man we knew
We depended on him, And he on us too

It's hard to explain the bond that we had
The loss of just one could make us all sad

We all saw things no one should ever see
Then we all got raging drunk on liberty

Our common fears and hurts and things we knew
Those were the ties we had, Those were the glue

We're all civilians now but none of us free
From the war we fight now in our memory

We're all still together when I sleep and dream
My buddies, My shipmates, My invincible team

The Innocents

We were so young
When we went there
Too green to know
But we sure tried

We lost our youth
We lost our friends
When we were men
But still we cried

Then we came home
Now all alone
Our friends all gone
So many died

We went to serve
We loved our land
Something went wrong
Our leaders lied

We now grow old
Our voices fade
But this we know
By God, we tried

The Lonely Marchers

The marchers in their endless rows
Pass faceless people no one knows
With banners waving, colors bright
Their eyes unseeing without sight
They march on by with cadence slow
As though they know just where to go
A rolling drum their only song
And with these men I march along
We've all been marching many years
Our faces streaked with dusty tears
Our fellow marchers all unknown
Our dogtags hidden, never shown
We're strangers all, But all the same
A common bond we all can claim
We are all prisoners of the mind
All marching for a key to find
Our loneliness a thing so real
We do not talk of how we feel
We march towards water at the well
Our march to end when we can tell

Scars Within

The bloody scars within my mind
That open now and then
Let loose the ancient memories
And I'm at war again

It's like a movie worn with age
With all the actors once well known
But now I only see a few
For the rest I cry and moan

For they're the ones that bled and died
And left me with my scars
And I wonder just how many more
Live thinking of their ghostly friends
That died in foreign wars

Veterans

Old men sitting at the bar
Trading tales of long ago
Of wars and battles they were in
Old memories causing tears to flow
One man sits shaking in his seat
A P.O.W. for three years
He mumbles how it used to be
Of brutal days and endless fears
One man lost a single eye
Another lost a leg somewhere
They all sit in this smoky bar
Remembering all the things they share
They're veterans of a fading past
They're here with friends to sit and drink
Their numbers fewer every year
Which causes them to sit and think
Oh yes, these were the lucky ones
The ones who sit here, in this bar
Each man a veteran of a war
And for his heart, a burning scar

Veteran's Day 1988

I walked with other vets today
On the streets of my hometown
And I saw lots of smiles today
Not one of us felt down
It made me proud to look around
And see these fighting men
To know this day was just for us
For the things we did back then
We're not just ordinary men
We all made history
What makes us special on this day
We fought for liberty
We sure looked like a motley bunch
But pride shone just the same
We didn't march, we kind of strolled
Cause some of us were lame
They put us at the very end
We followed all the rest
It was great just walking there
Among the very best
The guy beside me lost a leg
But he made it all the way
He made me proud to be a vet
On this, our special day

Veteran*s* Day 1999

This week the flags will wave again
We'll march down a city street
We'll try to keep the cadence
With grown old two left feet
We're veterans who have served our land
In places far and wide
Today we will be smiling
We won't show the hurt inside
The land that we all fought for
Is changing day by day
The people just don't seem to care
As their freedoms slip away
The Constitution was once sacred
A document held dear
Our founding fathers gave to us
A message once so clear
Now lying is accepted
And other things as bad
But we will show our smiles today
Pretend that we are glad
We will be with our brothers
And yes, our sisters too
We, ones who wore the uniform
And kept our honor true
We fought to keep this country free
Were our battles all in vain
My land, My country 'Tis of thee
Can we be free again

To Be A Veteran

It sure is nice to be a veteran
Of the wars that came our way
We don't need movies or T.V. shows
The real wars plague us day to day
The scenes are all real, no actors needed
Long lost buddies take their place
They are the ones who caught the big one
And now they're ghosts without a face
Look at all the fun we're having
Trying to place a face and name
To the friends who did not make it
To not remember and feel shame
Did Sergeant York and Audie Murphy
Feel this aching to the bone
I'm sure they did, for they were veterans
Their deeds were written, their souls unknown
I know they must have felt the heartache
Relived some memories in the night
Woke up sweating, heart a pounding
Try to scream with all their might
Yeah, it's nice to be a veteran
To be alive to tell the tale
But listen closely to our silence
And you may hear our silent wail

Wounded

How many of us have been wounded
Without shedding one drop of blood
And if all of us started crying
Our tears would cause a flood
Our wounds are deep within us
And the scars are in our mind
As we search the world around us
For the peace we'll never find
And we look for others like us
The only ones to give support
And we've closed our mind to others
And they cannot breach our fort
And we talk of anything but battle
That is one thing always near
But to bring it in the open
We just can't, it brings us fear
We were there and saw what happened
Saw our friends and buddies bleed
We were helpless as they died there
Couldn't help them in their need
So we walk around still wounded
Knowing that we'll never heal
And we hide the wounds within us
And no one knows just how we feel

Korea Olympics

The sun rose on a different scene
In nineteen eighty eight
The competition fierce again
But this time without hate
And Seoul saw many flags again
And people from afar
But this time they were there by choice
And not because of war
Each day the medals were presented to
The winners of that day
The losers were all left alive
There was no hell to pay
What a difference from so long ago
When no one thought of gold
Just stay alive another day
In good old wartime Seoul
So some of us looked at the games
And remembered with a tear
All the ones we lost back then
But that was another year

Korean Day And China Night

Can you remember way back then
When we were young, And fighting men

Our country sent us far away
To live our lives from day to day

We had our sorrows and our joys
We fought like men, but we were boys

We lost our friends, and then made new
So many men and yet so few

We drank and swore and acted tough
The times were cruel, the times were rough

It seemed like it would never end
Our minds were close to "Round the bend"

The days dragged by so very slow
How we survived, I'll never know

But sometimes music eased our fright
I still remember "*China Night*"

A foreign song, But oh so right
Korean day, And "*China Night*"

Forgotten war, That's what they say
But "*China Night*" won't go away

I've still got memories, So it seems
And "*China Night*" still fills my dreams

The Eight Hundred

My country, my land, my home far away, I'll never see you again.
I worked for you, fought for you, and now I'm living in pain.
It was not all the fighting, cause that was expected, although
it really was bad.
And being a prisoner, being cold, always hungry, didn't bring on
feeling hopeless and sad.
There were more than eight hundred, we were sold to the Russians,
we were young and basically strong.
Out of Korea, to the land of the bear, and the start of a terrible
wrong.
Although it was known, our own president knew, we were listed
as forever lost.
Our families cried, while our government lied, and kept secret
the terrible cost.
We were over eight hundred, and most of us died, after all it's
been forty long years.
But somewhere out there, there are some who still care, and weep
silently frustrated tears.
If there is a God, I'm not sure anymore, how could He allow
this to be?
Don't desert me, please find me, I may still be alive, please
listen to my forty year plea?

Tony

Tony had to climb his hill
It was a thing he had to do
He'd passed some wounded coming down
He felt the need to help those few

But Tony was sorely wounded
And they wouldn't let him go
So in his mind he climbs that hill
To help those guys he used to know

Today I was told he'd climb no more
Because Tony up and died
Today I lost another friend
Today I almost cried

Battle Hardened Vet

I saw the bitter lines around his mouth
And his eyes were hard and cold
I could see he'd been to hell and back
A battle hardened vet who fit the mold
Back in fifty he was there
When the devil came to visit and stayed awhile
Too few, So ill equipped, They had to fight
He lost a friend with every mile
Some were captured and tied with wire
A terrible way for a man to die
And some got killed just sitting there
Too worn out and tired to even cry
He got pushed back to near Pusan
Where the generals said *"run no more"*
So on the Naktong he made his stand
And that's where he started evening the score
By the end of fifty he was way up north
When the Chinese took a hand
And the mud and snow ran red with blood
While war raged through the land
Then he left the frozen Yalu
And he moved back south to Seoul
With the Chinese close behind him
The terrible winter took it's toll
In fifty one the war continued
It was still there in fifty two
In fifty three it was a stalemate
In July it would be through
By now he was so very lonely
He knew he'd never have a friend again

His old friends gone they died while fighting
To think of them brought only pain
So now he lives a lonely remnant
Forgotten man, Forgotten War
And no one knows how bad he's wounded
For no one there can see the scar
So he may look like he is bitter
And his eyes look hard and cold
For he's been waiting forty years now
He wants the stories to be told
He wants the war to be remembered
To honor all of those who fell
To think of all those we lost there
In Korea—Or was it hell

Brilliant Light

I sat and looked up at the sky
And saw a brilliant light
It sparkled with a million points
And almost burned my sight
I thought, Oh yes this must be it
The star we've waited for
The star of peace to light our world
And end this endless war
Shine in our hearts and give us hope
That tomorrow we'll be free
From fear and hunger and our hates
And give us sight to see
No man is different from the rest
Not one man is the best
We're really all one family
We all need peace and rest
Oh God I hope the light will stay
To shine through coming years
To shine into our very souls
And wipe away our fears
For my own part to keep the light
To all mankind I say
Please join with me and feel the love
On this our Christmas day

Korea

We didn't do much talking
We didn't raise a fuss
But Korea really happened
So please—Remember us
We all just did our duty
But we didn't win or lose
A victory was denied us
But we never got to choose
We all roasted in the summer
In the winter, damn near froze
Walking back from near the Yalu
With our blackened frozen toes
Like the surf the chinks kept coming
With the bugles in the night
And we fired into their masses
Praying for the morning light
All of us just had to be there
And so many of us died
But now we're all but half forgotten
No one remembers how we tried
We grow fewer with the years now
And we still don't raise a fuss
But Korea really happened
So please—*Remember us*

In 1991 I went back to Korea on a revisit trip. There were 28 of us and ten men brought their wives. We were taken all over on tours, and on one day visited Pan Mun Jom, where the truce was signed in 1953. It was an eery feeling being there and having North Korean soldiers keeping an eye on us with their binoculars. The photo above was taken when we visited the Korean War Museum, and we were treated to meeting a kindergarten class of Korean kids. The thing that brought tears to our eyes was when elderly Koreans would walk up to us, bow, and say "Thank You". Something we never heard in our own country.

Korea On T.V.

Last night I watched
Surprised and pleased that I could see
At last, For once
The Korean war was on T.V.

In one short hour
The story told what happened there
So long ago
It's hard to find someone to care

It wasn't Nam
With all it's jungles filled with fear
But like in Nam
The end result was not so clear

We fought so hard
So many died, So many lost
We did not win
We did not lose, But at what cost

I'm still alive
And so are others who were there
Forgotten war
Forgotten men, No one to care

The High

I felt like a god one time
But the feeling did not last
I tried to bring it back again
But it's fading in the past

I felt I had great power
The power of life and death
But the feeling was so fleeting
It was gone by my next breath

It was brought about by gunfire
The roar and all the flame
If I live to be a hundred
I will never feel the same

It was probably all the danger
Feeling naked and exposed
Taking fire from heavy weapons
Not knowing what I feared the most

Being killed is always final
But being maimed is always worse
Facing life a helpless cripple
I could think of nothing worse

And then the order came to fire
And all our guns fired with a roar
It is then that I felt godlike
And I felt my spirit soar

It only lasted but a short time
And then I felt return to fear
But for a moment I felt godlike
But maybe t'was God I felt so near

Lonely

Lonely country
Lonely roads
Lonely days
And lonely miles

Lonely faces
Lonely people
Lonely music
And lonely smiles

Lonely towns
Lonely cities
Lonely clouds
In lonely skies

Lonely graveyard
Lonely grace
Lonely bugle
When lonely dies

Lonely Places

I love those far off places
Where I can be alone
Those places filled with sighing wind
And moonlight on the stone
Where I look up and see the stars
Against the sky so black
And wonder once again the why
Of my life's burning track
No one can see if too much light
Wipes starlight from the sky
No one can hear with too much talk
No matter how you try
You have to hear the silence
To hear the words not said
You have to tread the unseen path
To see what lies ahead
So I seek lonely places
Those places for my kind
And let the lonesome sighing wind
Blow troubles from my mind

The Grenade

A metal casing dull and green

Explosive power time machine

It's power harnessed by a pin

A lethal package hid within

It has no mind, so it can wait

It doesn't love, it doesn't hate

It's just another hand grenade

Designed to maim when it was made

And with some men it's just the same

Although they feel and take the blame

And though once taught to kill and hurt

They now leave teardrops in the dirt

Like the grenade they are man built

But they are men and feel the guilt

A lethal package hid within

As long as nothing pulls the pin

The Call

The blood of men flows ever out
As raging rivers to the sea
There seems to be an endless source
From long lost memory
The young men come to volunteer
To shed their blood once more
They've heard the call to bleed again
Upon some distant shore
Why is the call to die so strong
That men will heed the call
Or do they think they're not the ones
Who'll take the final fall
It's always someone else who dies
Not we who volunteer
We think we'll never be the one
And laugh to hide our fear
But deep within our inner souls
We know we may be wrong
That death may be around the turn
Our life may not be long
But never mind we heard the call
We line up in our ranks
And a grateful nation will be there
To give us all their thanks
They'll build for us a monument
Young boys will come to stare
And they will be the next to go
To shed their blood somewhere

Talking

What the hell do you want me to say
When the words stick in my throat
Can't you see that it hurts like hell
And my silence is my moat
I've been hiding in my castle
For a lot of lonely years
Building my walls ever higher
Trying to hide from all my fears
When I write I'm really talking
What I do when I'm in need
Don't just see the words I'm writing
Between the lines you have to read
You don't know how hard I find it
Just to tell like some guys do
But I suspect that all the talkers
Are not many, just a few
I sit and listen, getting shaky
My nerves on fire from what I feel
Then I go back, to many years now
And the memories are just like real
I know these talks are to be healing
But at this time they hurt like hell
So please bear with me when I'm silent
And when I'm ready I will tell

Sharing The Load

You may not want to share the burden

Of that heavy memory load

Always thinking there's a finish

That there is an end to every road

But remember there are others

With a burden, just like you

Loaded down with bad old memories

And they're haunted just like you

Heavy loads become much lighter

When they're given out to share

When you talk to others like you

And you know the others care

You will never know no burden

Heavy memories stick around

But share the load to ease the burden

Walk with others you have found

Semper Fi Chat

I feed my soul with conversation
A talk with men who were there too
Who left their friends in far off places
The men who now become so few

Our gray hair is an indication
That we are now among the old
Our talks revolve around an era
When we were young and oh so bold

We talk of war and talk of pleasure
We talk of friends who are now gone
Our martial past a fine honed memory
But now, oh God, we're so alone

We are now strangers in our country
Civilians do not think the way we do
So when we talk, we're back together
The ones who went, the proud, the few

Scared??? — Not Me!

What's that hairy thing up in my throat

It's as fuzzy as an old mink coat

I'm glad it's small and doesn't grow

But how it got there I don't know

It may be a symptom of the flu

Cause I'm also shaking through and through

I had all my shots before I got to this place

So what is causing that twitch in my face

I've never quite felt these feelings before

And I sure as hell don't want anymore

That hairy thing is now right near my tongue

The guys holler *"swallow"*, cause that is your bung

Remembrance

Remembrance flows through heart and soul

The rushing thoughts a mighty stream

Remembering things from long ago

And deep within a silent scream

Their faces crowd into my dreams

Of those that left but are so near

As vibrant beings once alive

They whisper poems in my ear

I am the hand that grips the pen

I am their vehicle of trust

And when they're with me telling tales

They're all alive, no longer dust

I cry for them with pen and ink

And pray for them on bended knees

But I can't help, I'm all alone

And weep my tears that no one sees

R And R

R and R was a wonderful time
It made heroes of us all
It was a time to lie like hell
To fool yourself and feel real tall
We hit the beach, Dry as a bone
And tried to drink the whole town dry
Try as we might, We never did
But damn, We had to try
We fell in love, Or was it lust
At least four times a night
And when the M.P.'s cruised the scene
We all got out of sight
We really liked those Mama-Sans
They treated us real nice
An ice cold beer, A real hot bath
Now who could call that vice?
We spent our dough and did it all
We sure as hell had fun
Yes R and R was a wonderful time
When all is said and done
Except for the headache the following day
When we faced that morning sun
I swear you guys, **"*never again*"**
But maybe just once for fun

"Nevvah Happin G. I. Joe"

When I was over in Westpac
Where English was quite rare
It was great to go on R and R
Without a worry or a care
We all had lots of money
MPC's or local dough
And I was hoping that I wouldn't hear

"Nevvah Happin G.I. Joe"

The girls were always friendly
And they knew lots more than we
They knew exactly what our orders were
And sometimes that bothered me
So sometimes I'd try to ask them
How anyone of them could know
And they'd answer with a little smile

"Nevvah Happin G.I. Joe"

But now those wars are over
At least I think that is the case
But i still remember all those times
Sometimes tears run down my face
Yeah, those wars are really over
At least I hope that's so
But I still know what those girls all said

"Nevvah Happin G.I. Joe"

Yeah, it's true my wars are over
I'm now old, my hair turns gray
But I still remember things that happened

All those things won't go away
And in my dreams I hear those words
And they're like "I told you so"
I hear all those girls still telling me

"Nevvah Happin G.I. Joe"

Catch 22

You have a problem
And now you're an old time vet
So you go to the V.A.
For some help to get
You walk into an office
And there they take your name
Then you wait with other vets
With them, discuss your claim
Your name is finally called
And you walk right in
But what happens next
Is a goddamn sin
They ask a lot of questions
About why you're there
But it's really about money
That they really care
They ask about insurance
If you've done really well
But not about your problems
Or if you've been to hell
So if you've saved some money
And your income is too high
You've got to have insurance
For them to even try
But if you're retired
And Champus pays the doc
You don't need insurance
That's like two feet in a sock
But the V.A. just can't help
Unless you're covered all the way

Cause you're just a goddamn vet
And they wish you'd go away
I sure as hell don't want their money
A little help is all I need
But they see me as a veteran
Another asshole filled with greed
So I'll live with all my problems
The ones that never go away
Kiss my ass you V.A. assholes
that's one thing this vet can say

Goodbye

Goodbye you guys, goodbye
I'm standing here
With a hand salute
But what I want to do
Is cry
They've got you
In those boxes
Covered up
With the red, white, and blue
You've got your transfer orders
Now goddamn it
I want to cry
I know
I have to hold it
And I look
As hard as nails
But damn
I'm going to miss you
If they'd only
Let me cry
We're all standing
At attention
And the bugler's
Playing taps
I sure don't feel much
Like a man today
Goodbye you guys
Goodbye

My Soul

Somewhere my soul is still at war

I cannot seem to find my peace

The ghosts still wander through my head

Their whispers to me never cease

It's not just men I used to know

There were so many there that died

Although I grieve, my heart is torn

In all those years I haven't cried

The wars been over for so long

And yet it seems like yesterday

Sometimes I feel I've never left

The deep dark hurt is here to stay

The enemy is now my own mind

The only place I cannot hide

From all the ghosts that wander there

And remind me that I've never cried

My Neighbor

You don't want to meet my neighbor
He's not friendly don't you know
He likes to take my buddies
Even when they don't want to go

He doesn't care how young they are
Or why, Or when, Or where
And he doesn't care just how it's done
And when they're hurt, He's there

He lives among us all the time
He's the champion of his game
No matter what you try or do
He'll be the winner just the same

He loves big wars and small ones too
He loves them way too much
He hovers round the battlefields
And many feel his touch

I know I'm not supposed to call him
He's just a thing called death
But a lot of us have watched him work
And felt his icy breath

He took my friends and others too
The list is way too long
I know he's death, He's just a thing
But what he did—Was wrong!

Memorial Day 1997

One day a year we stop to think
of all the ones we've lost
We never stop to realize
just what the wars have cost
We have parades, and wave some flags
and think of wars gone by
We stand in graveyards with the rest
and we may even cry
The bugle sounds as taps is played
then the honor guards salute
Another day has come and gone
and the bugle now is mute
The little flags will wave again
in just another year
We'll think back like we did before
and shed another tear
How many more will bleed and die
and then lie here so still
Not telling of the pain they had
upon some distant hill
We must remember all year long
not just a single day
We must remember through the year
not just memorial day

Lonely I Remain

For all my life I've been alone
And lonely I remain
No matter how I cry for help
Alone, I feel the pain

I never had much family
We never were real close
As soon as I was old enough
The wandering life I chose

I spent nine years with Uncle Sam
I served him, always true
I won't forget those wondrous years
When I wore navy blue

I wore my uniform with pride
And funny—I felt free
And all those guys I lived among
They were my family

Then I got hitched, I had to leave
The pay was not enough
I had to face civilian life
And at first it was real tough

The years have gone, I'm growing old
The leisure years ahead
I should be happy with my life
But doubt still fills my head

I've tried to get through to my wife
My thoughts to her explain
But all my life I've been alone
And lonely I remain

Just Another Day

Today was just another day
A day like all the rest
But today I got a job to do
Or was it just a test
All the pieces were in plastic jars
And the pieces were of men
These pieces were to go back home
To where they lived back then
I had to make some bodies
And add the proper weight
The folks back home would never know
How awful was their fate
Just box them up to ship them out
That's the thing I had to do
These were men who'd fought the fight
And now their lives were through
But what it did to men like me
No one gave that a thought
We were survivors, really tough
From the battle we just fought
Tomorrow we might fight again
And tomorrow we might die
But for god's sake, please don't ship me home
Unless I'm whole, and not a lie
I don't want to go in pieces
Bloody bits of what was me
I would rather be remembered
As a whole man memory

Invisible Medal

The invisible medal
Was awarded today
It was given for reason
That no one can say
We were told to be silent
About what happened that day
We were not in the area
We were not in the fray
No one got hurt there
Not one person died
At least that's the story
Oh God, how they lied
So they awarded a medal
But why, I don't know
If anyone asks me
It's only for show
I can't talk about it
I can not tell why
And when pressed for details
I'm forced to lie
So why did they give it
And why can't I say
The invisible medal
Was awarded today

Forgotten

Forgotten war, Forgotten men
They fought and bled and died, and then
They came back home to what? I ask
Forget what happened? No easy task

Where are the people who understand?
There must be some in this great land
You close your heart and close your mind
And hope to find some of your kind

They are the only ones who know
Of mental battles that grow and grow
Please let me ease this awful pain
Please let me live alive and sane

I feel so naked when I tell
Of my own journey into hell
Please let me ease this awful pain
Please let me live alive and sane

Evening Sun

I watched the evening sun go down
As day turned into night
Then all the little puffs of smoke
Turned into balls of light
They curved across the evening sky
It was a sight to see
But somehow I felt quite upset
When they curved right at me
At celebrations way back home
We shot off fireworks too
But now I'm in this foreign land
With a different point of view
The fireworks here are not the same
They have a different goal
What all these balls of light can do
Puts fear into my soul
How can it be so beautiful
And yet be sudden death
Will my eyes sparkle with those lights
When I sigh with my last breath
I look at others with me
Do they see the beauty too
Or do they only see the awful side
What those balls of light can do

Coming Home

I have been so many places
I have seen so many faces
I have traveled far and wide
So very long

I think of all the things I've done
Things so very far from fun
And the reason for those things
Were they so wrong?

Now I'm a stranger where I go
Wish to God it wasn't so
But I know deep in my heart
I don't belong

Called

There are men called by their country

Whose acts in war bring them some fame

But acts in war and acts in peacetime

Although in faith, may bring some shame

For God and Country, we're asked to do things

Some things so dark we cannot name

And then alone we seek for answers

And dream our dreams of hellfire flame

We cannot talk, our minds a prison

Our crippled thoughts have pulled up lame

Our anguished cries go toward the heavens

Oh God! Am I the only one to blame?

Buddies

What happened to all my buddies
Did they all just disappear
Have they died or gone to other places
Don't they know that I'm still here

I wish I knew all of their real names
Not all the nicknames which I knew
Then I could really try to find them
And maybe they are looking too

I travel far with eyes wide open
You never know, so I'll keep trying
The years go by, we're all much older
It won't be long, we'll all be dying

Buddies of mine where are you hiding
You were there when the sun still shone
Buddies of mine please try to find me
Yeah, damn it all, I'm so alone

Boats

He was one hell of a sailor
A BoatswainsMate all the way through
Crossed hooks on the sleeve of his jumper
The job real men chose to do
In a storm with all hatches battened
He was topside to see all was secure
He double checked all of the tiedowns
Then again just to make sure
You might say he had just one failing
He really liked wearing his whites
He was one sharp looking sailor
On a liberty, and seeing the sights
But at sea when we sailed into battle
Dungarees is what we all wore
And if you were killed in the battle
You'd never wear whites anymore
In his case we made an exception
When his life was ended one day
We made sure he was properly dressed
He was special, what more can you say
The crew all stood by the railing
And the Skipper had a few words to say
We saluted and stood at attention
When his body was tilted away
No more G.Q.'s he would answer
No more bloody battles and fights
But when "Boats" left us forever
By GOD, he was wearing his whites

Comfort

Comfort is just being with friends
Or with people who know where you've been
And know that you dream, about some of the places
And sometimes go back again

The nice thing is, they're all just like you
They have known the bad and the good
You don't have to hide the things in your mind
Cause with them it's all understood

And then you give comfort, and listen to them
When they talk of all of their pain
So you listen real close, and laugh when you can
Yeah, comfort is hard to explain

The Wall

He walked up to the long black wall

To look for names of men he knew

But all he saw was faces

Their features etched into the stone

He saw them standing all alone

So silent in their places

The rain came down to wet the stone

They now appeared as flesh and blood

Their eyes left tear filled traces

He'd come three thousand miles to see

To say goodbye and then feel free

But all he saw was faces

The Lucky K.I.A.

The years flow by as water in a stream
And like the boulders in that stream
Some memories will always stay
As I think back my eyesight blurs
From all the things my memories stirs
And I reflect upon the lucky K.I.A.
One of us among those sent
One of us who always went
And now the one who'll always stay
He said he'd never be the one
He was there just for the fun
The war was just a game to play
His eyes, not once, had shed a tear
He walked upright and without fear
And never thought to kneel and pray
And not like us, he loved the war
And always knew what he was fighting for
While we just lived from day to day
Inside he hid an awful dread
A fate worse than being dead
but the lucky stiff was K.I.A., thank God not M.I.A

So many of us are still M.I.A., and don't even know it.
Will we ever make it back?

The New Ones Are The First To Go

New seeds sprout forth
To face the day
Each bursting forth
In brave array
Not knowing yet
The death they face
And die they will
In any case
There are young men
Just like the seeds
Who's hearts are filled
with mighty deeds
Who will attack
When told to go
And like the seeds
The truth they'll know
There's always some
Who will survive
Who will mature
And be alive
See the young
So bold and brave
Who'll never ask
Just what they gave
The new ones come
The new ones go
For they can't hear
I told you so

The Memorial

We tried, We tried

Oh God, We tried

So we could be here too

And walk around

Remembering

And look for names we knew

Our lives were lost

So far away

Upon a distant shore

But we are here

In memory

As you read our names

Once more

Remember us

Remember us!

Although we're truly gone

Remember us, as we once were

And not just names

In stone

The Creeping Crud

The creeping crud, the creeping crud

That stuff was sure a bitch

No matter what you tried to do

There was that constant itch

I tried Quinsana powder

And the Corpsman gave me salve

But nothing touched the creeping crud

Not even close by half

The south end of the China sea

Is where I got my case

Just one more goddamn reason

I did not like that place

There's sure a lot to remember

And forget, If you just could

But one thing I'll always remember

That goddamn creeping crud

Some Perimeters Are A Scary Sonofabitch

There are some things within my life
That I may never mention
But if I never talk
How can I ease the tension
I know of others like me
Who have done some things the same
And after all these many years
Do they also feel some shame
Oh God, why did I do it
At the time it seemed so right
It was for God and country
I walked deep, into the night
Now I'm trapped, my night unending
Not one whisper can I say
If my wife knew all the details
Would she ever let me stay?
I'll never talk, of that I'm certain
There are too many lives at stake
They have to live in other places
I must be silent for their sake
So I write poems, my way of talking
Of things I cannot say
And I dream dreams of God and country
And I wish they'd go away
Only one man I could trust
Now there's no one

Ribbons

Rows and rows of ribbons
Each one with a meaning of its own
They tell a story of the wearer
Of all the places he has known
His ribbons say he's a hero
No decorations, only trash
But he remembers where he got them
And not one he'd trade for cash
He only did his duty
And he went when asked to go
He never let his buddies down
And he never once said no
He was just a part of something
And he did more than his share
But he never was a hero
As for that he didn't care
He just did what he was told to
And he did that very well
Doing things that he was trained for
In the bright hot flames of hell
So now he's back with only ribbons
To remind him he was there
But he never was a hero
And there's no one left to care

Names

I stood and faced
The long black wall
And not one name
I could recall
John M. this
And Frank C. that
Where were the names?
Where were they at?
Where was Buddha?
And where was Slim?
Robert S. Johnson?
I didn't know him
Where was Gunner?
Where was Sparks?
One went to hell
The other to sharks
Goddamn my memory
Goddamn it to hell
I knew their nicknames
I knew them well
Now they are gone
Their names on a wall
Not one goddamn nickname
And I can't recall

Overseas

How many men went overseas
To fight on a foreign shore
And some to die while fighting there
To sleep forever more

But what of those that stayed behind
As prisoners of the foe
Those P.O.W.'s and M.I.A.'s
How many, Do we know?

How can we stand so silently
And never say a word
We must speak out, Us veterans
Our voices must be heard

So we will march from shore to shore
To send a message clear
We want our brothers left behind
We want our brothers *Here!*

We'll gather veterans through the land
Our army will grow strong
And maybe then our government
Will right this awful wrong

Phantom Panel

Phantom panels at the wall
Like stealth aircraft in the air
Look real close, but you won't see
But I tell you that they're there
To find the panels close your eyes
Then look left, before sixty three
The phantom panels start to glow
And phantom figures you will see
These are the men who died unknown
Whose records show they never went
These are the men with tales untold
Who did not know why they were sent
You may not like the bloody truth
And then the panels fade away
But some of us were really there
For all of us the panels stay
No signs of glory will we see
A bitter silence fills the air
But we will see the trace of tears
Of gallant men who aren't there
So when we visit at the wall
To pay respects to those who fell
We look for phantoms to the left
Those men still in an unknown hell

Just Another Vet

I met another vet last night
A vet like you and me
Whose memories compare to ours
The ones we want to flee

As veterans go, this one was small
But large for what was done
This vet saw blood and guts and death
And never touched a gun

Without this vet where would we be
To help us in our hurt
To hold our hand and cleanse the wound
And wipe away the dirt

Can we forget this vet?
No way I'm sure that's true
This vet gave us a chance to live
Our lives for me and you

She was a *woman* in the war
But like us, can't you see
I met another vet last night
A vet like you and me

I Saw

I saw the memorial
With statues of men
And they were all soldiers
To remember back then
When war was a-raging
In a land far away
And our men were dying
In that bloody fray
But never a sailor
Do I ever see
And they were there also
On land and at sea
They used their big guns
To help those ashore
The ships brought replacements
Food, ammo, and more
The carrier air wings
Were there day and night
And sailors as corpsmen
Were in the thick of the fight
So why not a sailor
On the monuments too
They also fought bravely
Let's give them their due

Half A World Away

I ate steak and shrimp tonight

A meal fit for a king

When someone half a world away

Did not eat a thing

I'll sleep between clean sheets tonight

While half a world away

Another vet will pray to God

To ask for one more day

There is no war, our leaders say

There's no condition red

While far away a vet will sleep

On bamboo for a bed

No M.I.A.'s our leaders say

They say it loud and strong

And just a half a world away

A vet could prove them wrong

Bamboo Bars

When I was young and life was fun

I used to jump and play and run

Then I grew older, thought of cars

But never once of bamboo bars

I couldn't wait to turn eighteen

To graduate my biggest dream

I'd reach far out beyond the stars

But never thought of bamboo bars

I thought my life was far too tame

And overseas there burned a flame

So off I went to do my thing

Not knowing all the hurt 'twould bring

And now I'm left with only scars

And watch the stars through bamboo bars

Emotions

It's cold, and all night the fireflies,
On the far off shore, have been blinking
Oh God, I'm so tired, I'm so scared
And all through the night I've been thinking

Will today be the same as the day we just had,
And the day we just had just before
If it is, Oh my God, I don't know if I can
But I know that I must, one day more

I can see all the smoke, and hazy gray hills
There's lightning and thunder, not a cloud in the sky
I hear trains come by rumbling, and sometimes a
Moaning, and white balls of fire fly by

I know they can see us, we're such a big target
From all the splashes I know that they've tried
What the hell is the matter, I'm shaking all over
Why am I so frightened, have I lost my pride

My headphones are crackling, the order comes screaming
Commence with the firing and give them some hell
My whole world is thunder, I've lost all my fear
It's my turn to be killing, I crawl out of my shell

The noise is horrendous and everyone's shouting
The five inch concussions slam into my guts
I'm no longer tired, oh God I feel happy
But I hope these emotions won't drive us all nuts

Dreams

Silent voices, silent screams
Faceless memories fill my dreams
Why do they return to haunt me
When they left so long ago
Ghostly visions all aglow
I did not cry then, when it happened
I've never shed a single tear
And their names still elude me
Although once they were so clear
Are they trying to tell me something
When they're with me in the night
Making me join in their dying
Making me join their fright
They can make my heart go pounding
They can fill my nights with fear
They can make me wake up sweating
But can they make me shed a tear

Corpsman

Corpsman! Corpsman!
A cry that I hate
Sometimes they're handy
Sometimes too late
How do they hear me
Through all of the noise
When I'm almost crying
A crack in my voice
Oh God, I'm so helpless
What the hell do I do
So I holler Corpsman
And hope he gets through
He's just got to make it
My buddies a mess
I don't think he'll make it
I've got to confess
I keep crying Corpsman
And hope that I'm wrong
Oh please hear me Corpsman
Oh please don't be long

Back Then

My dreams back then were oh so clear
Of round eye broads, and steaks, and beer
Of milk, and real eggs on my plate
To do without, that was my fate
There were lots of things I didn't mind
But a glass of milk, I could not find
Ten thousand miles away from home
I dreamt of milk with a head of foam
To gulp it down and drink real fast
Or sip it slow and make it last
Then eat my steak with eggs on top
Instead of eating all this slop
Then finish it off with real ice cream
A fabulous meal in a fabulous dream
Then I came home from far away
And drank lots of milk, every day
I ate steak and eggs with butter and toast
All the things I missed the most
The flavor was there but it wasn't the same
Just being back home was probably to blame
But I still remember and my throat gets real tight
When a cold glass of milk would have been a delight

Weapons

There are many type of weapons

But the ones that hurt the most

Are the weapons made of memories

And the deadly midnight ghost

Not all wounds are red and bloody

There are wounds that touch the mind

These are wounds that always fester

They're the never healing kind

Why are we who've done our duty

Plagued by wounds that never heal

Made by weapons of our memories

Which are worse then lead and steel

Where No One Cares

We are the ones
The ones that went
We left our homes
We left our land
To fight so far away
We didn't know
How it would be
We couldn't know
How we would be
Uncertain and afraid
And acting unafraid
But we would change
From soft to hard
And learn the ways
To stay alive
While others died
From not knowing
Or was it luck
Live meant going back
Back to our home
Back to our land
Where no one cared
But we did
Cause we remembered
How we remembered
Mostly at night
When we go back
We're there again
And feel again
Our hidden fears

And meet our friends
Who did not learn
Or had no luck
But they still talk
And they still walk
In our mind
And sometimes call
For us to join
Them in their sleep
So we must change
Grow diamond hard
To live again
As we once were
Back to our home
Back to our land
Where no one cares
Where no one cares

Two Words

There were two words that said a lot
Regardless of how bad things got
And when the situation was real hot

"Fuck It"

A guy would get a dear John note
And he'd drink till he would almost float
But these helping words he knew by rote

"Fuck It"

Your best buddy could be damn near dead
From a piece of shrapnel in his head
Remember the last words that he said

"Fuck It"

Things got so bad you couldn't sleep
And worse than that you couldn't weep
But those two words you'd always keep

"Fuck It"

You counted all the day to go
And then found out it wasn't so
It was a real big shock to know

"Fuck It"

So now were out, but the memories stay
And the goddamn dreams won't go away
And all that I can really say is

"Fuck It"

Transferred

A friend of mine got transferred today

He didn't even have a chance to say goodbye

Before he left for a duty station far away

Once he was a gun ship pilot, Marine Corps, Semper Fi

But a NVA gun clipped his wings

And worse than that, he couldn't fly

He became a civilian, but not in his mind

He was still wearing wings and coming in low

Firing his guns and protecting his kind

He was tied to the ground now, no place to be

And he longed to be flying

To be up in the sky, to be happy and free

So now he got transferred and now he can fly

I hope he is happy wherever he is

With wings of gold, way up in the sky

Goodbye Bob, We'll miss you

"Unnatural Causes" A Film

I watched a movie about all of the vets
Exposed to defoliant spray
And I thought of all of the vets
That are hurting and dying each day
This isn't a movie we watch on TV
This is real and it's not just a tale
They are blind, they are crippled
And some slightly nuts
They are prisoners of hurt with no bail
They all did their duty away from this land
And sometimes it was too much to bear
It's hard to watch buddies die in the dirt
And wondering if there's someone to care
Then going home happened, it was a great day
Leaving all of the misery behind
But the war never left, especially at night
It's almost like losing your mind
And some left some pieces, no longer whole
And some are dying real slow
And they're lying in beds all over this land
With wheelchairs that no longer go
So I think of the movie, and think of the war
And I think of the friends I have lost
And I wonder how many just watching that film
Remember just what it all cost

Ham and Mothers

I loved the names we gave our food
Although some names were downright lewd
One thing for sure the stuff was light
That made a difference in a fight

The rations now are MRE's
The rations then were mostly "C"s
There were some good, and some were bad
But damn it all, that's all we had

And there were times that you could swap
Cause there were guys who loved the slop
At every meal came time to trade
It was a fun game that we played

There was one ration we all know
I'll tell you now we loved it so
The one we really loved to eat
"Ham and Mothers" was the treat

Yes, lima beans were good for you
They manufacture methane gasses too
But if you think I'm selling sky
I'm just a vet, and never lie

Group Session

What the hell do you want me to say
When the words stick in my throat
Can't you see that it hurts like hell
And my silence is my moat
I've been hiding in my castle
For a lot of lonely years
Building my walls ever higher
Trying to hide from all my fears
When I write, I'm really talking
What I do, when I'm in need
Don't you see the words I'm writing
Between the lines you have to read
You don't know how hard I find it
Just to tell like some guys do
But I suspect that all the talkers
Are not many, just a few
I sit and listen, getting shaky
My nerves on fire from what I feel
Then I go back to many years now
And my memories are just like real
I know these talks are to be healing
But at this time they hurt like hell
So please bear with me when I'm silent
And when I'm ready, I will tell

The Nine

No matter where you are, or when
There are men who you can count on
These guys are there, no matter what
Not like a REMF who's gone

These are the guys who'll walk the point
And be there, come what may
These are the guys who'll share their RATS
And never ask for pay

But you have got to choose and pick
Get rid of all the chaff
No matter what your rank or rate
You've got to pick your staff

So be real careful who you pick
And then you'll be just fine
Remember what they've always said
"I say fuck em all, but nine

This poem is dedicated to Gary Chenett,
a serious grunt.
He told me, that there were always going to be nine to cover your ass and get you out
Six Pallbearers, two Road Guards, and a Sergeant
calling cadence

Land And Sea

He's just a dogface
I'm just a sailor
And I know
That I have it made
He lives in a foxhole
I live on a ship
And I sure as hell
Wouldn't trade
But sometimes things change
And sailors catch hell
After all
We're easy to see
There's no place to hide
On a quad forty
When the shrapnel
Is looking for me
I'll say this old buddy
You're probably right
On a ship
Things ain't so rough
But dogface or sailor
Some things are the same
Losing buddies
Will always be tough
So sailor or dogface
We all had our moments
In those places
That we had to roam
We all had our hopes
We all had a prayer
Please God
Just let me go home

The Storm

At sea, and far away from any shore, I felt the first change in the air. A feeling of unease wrapped itself around the ship, and imperceptible things began to occur in the surrounding sea, and the sky above, small things, and yet noticed by those to whom the sea was home. A check of the barometer, showed a rapid and steady falling of pressure, and from the wind direction the knowledge came that the ship was in the path of a storm.

A thousand howling, screaming, banshees, tearing and clawing at every vestige of things manmade. Salt spray blowing horizontally sanding things painted, and causing pain to unprotected flesh. The sea twisting in its agony of tumultuous violence, forming itself into huge shapes to overwhelm and drown all things in its path. The ship fighting for its life, its metal screeching and moaning in the agony of its battle. Metal parts breaking off, some to fly and disappear into oblivion, and others crashing into other metal parts to add to the cacophony of sounds. All movement now is in every plane conceivable. Up, down, and sideways become confused. Men, some too sick to care, and others fighting to save the ship, and themselves, thrown about as breaking balls on a pool table. Hatches warp and become inlets for streams of sea water, cascading down ladders to flood footlockers, short out electrical systems, and cause decks to become slides to hell. A day, a night, and then again, the storm maintains its assault. Its screams grow louder as it causes the sea to create mightier and mightier fists of water to pound and subjugate this metal thing heaving on its bosom, and then King Neptune relents. The ship and its crew have passed the ultimate of tests. The winds cease their howl of death, and the seas lose their maddened foaming crests and are satisfied to slide silently underneath the keel. We have been allowed to live ***this time!***

The Tie That Binds

Have you ever noticed that whenever some veterans, of some of our wars, get together, even if it's only a couple guys, they seem to have a bond. Sometimes very few words are exchanged and yet they seem to know about each other. This secret knowledge draws them together, and makes them brothers in a closed society. I don't think anyone will ever be able to analyze this phenomenon and come up with a completely factual explanation, it is just something that happens, but it is something which makes non members of that closed society try even harder to penetrate its secrets. Non members will be confused, and will mostly imagine what it is that makes a veteran a veteran. By definition, a veteran is someone, who has served his/her country in wartime, and this is an honorable definition, but unless a veteran has had experiences which have shocked him, frightened him and made him do things totally beyond his upbringing in a civilized and reasonable society, he won't be a member of that elusive closed society.

Experiences can be a devastating blow to everything a person was ever taught. In a world of rules and laws, you are by circumstance thrown into an arena of almost complete lawlessness where the art of simple survival becomes a primary goal. You are part of an indescribable scene of deprivation, pain, and death, under the constant threat of becoming a victim to the horrors surrounding you. Friends and acquaintances come and go, and soon it becomes too painful to even consider making another friend. In self defense you turn inward, and harden yourself to the things around you. You become so successful at this, that you develop an invisible wall, which nothing or anyone can penetrate. In the process you have taught yourself not to care, and to only concern yourself with your own safety. You learn to kill without the slightest hesitation, and you become very proficient and effective at eliminating whatever is a possible threat. You have become a professional.

After years of service to your country, you are now a civilian, and subject to the rules of a supposedly sane and civilized society. What was acceptable behavior is no longer acceptable and you are now an outcast in the very society which sent you away under the auspices of doing your duty to that society. Knowing where you have been, and guessing what you have had to do, you are no longer a fully accepted member of that society. Somehow you have become different, and like a trained tiger, someone to never fully trust. No one understands, and after the first expressions of sympathy for the terrible things you must have gone through, you are gradually forgotten. Your immediate family worries about your outbursts of intense rage, your sleep problems, your bouts with alcohol, and your difficulties in holding a job, but mostly they figure it is your problem and never ask too many questions. The survival techniques you have perfected are no longer of use, and you have become an amateur among people incapable of understanding and for the most part unwilling to help. The feelings of frustration and total despair causes you to think of terminating your existence, and worse of all the feelings of intense guilt begin to surface. You begin to question the things you did and the decisions you made and wonder if it could have been different.

Hey man, you have arrived. You are now a member of our "*Fuck-em-All Closed Society.*"

The Vet Center

Those people at the center
Are a real nice bunch of folks
They listen to our stories
And they listen to our jokes
They listen when we sit there
And don't have much to say
And try to help us bring
Some sunshine to our day
They listen when we're in a group
Or when we're all alone
And they listen when we're far away
To our stories hard as stone
They listen to our tales of war
That is no easy thing
The things we did when we were young
And the nightmares that they bring
Thank God that there are listeners
Who will listen when we talk
We will stay beside us every step
When back in time we walk

Those Left Behind

I walk with gods, I really do
Just don't get hurt, And so will you

Incoming rounds, The shit can fly
I'm scared as hell, But I'll get by

Oh Jesus Christ, A guy is hit
They can't touch me, I'm just not it

I have no friends, I just don't dare
Cause if I did, I'd have to care

If this is true please tell me why
When I think back, I want to cry

Just what the hell is wrong with me
A hard-shelled bastard can't you see

No way those guys we left behind
Can make my heart be soft and kind

Or is it true, It's all a lie
Cause when I think, I want to cry

I walked with gods high on a hill
Those left behind are with me still

To Survive

He was sent just like the rest
And he knew he'd have to do his best

To survive

He was trained and knew the ropes
Full of fears and full of hopes

To survive

He learned to live when others died
When some gave up he always tried

To survive

The rounds came in the shrapnel flew
And he was one of just a few

To survive

And now he's back, He kept his vow
The rules are changed and he's asking how

To survive

He's in the world and has to earn
But things have changed and he has to learn

To survive

Now memories come to torment his mind
And he needs help from his own kind

To survive

He needs support and he needs to tell
He needs to leave his private hell

To survive

He has to face his problems day to day
And like other vets he'll find a way

To survive

Warrior

I hear the ancient voices calling
With sword in hand they wait for me
Ancestral blood within me hailing
Tall sailing ships upon the sea
We once sailed far upon the ocean
Brought fear into the hearts of men
They now tell tales about our daring
Our singing swords we used back then
We sailed far south where men grew darker
We fought whole armies for their gold
Stood toe to toe with helmets gleaming
But they withdrew, while we were bold
Ancestral memories still come weaving
Old runes inscribed upon my mast
The spar which holds my soul unfurling
The secrets of my ancient past
Valhalla waits, a warriors heaven
The Gods have set a place for me
The Valkyrie will lift me skyward
When my ship burns upon the sea

What Is A War

A war is not just the dying
It's not just the guys being killed
Cause when the goddamn thing's over
The theaters have got to be filled
A war must have lots of glamour
With controversy a must
The enemy soldiers all rapists
With killing and dying and lust
A war can make lots of money
For people who are in that game
And as long as there's plenty of profit
There'll be many who think just the same
A war must always have glory
With medals, and honors, and fame
Don't take pictures of all of the dying
Of all of the blind and the lame
A war can be really disgusting
The wounds, all the blood, and the smell
The moans, and the screams, and the crying
Just call it a preview of hell

Where?

I woke up on the gun mount
To face an eerie sight
A strange foreboding landscape
Had crept up in the night
It was a land I dreaded
With fear and death nearby
Mist rising on the mountains
With dark clouds in the sky
I saw some bright white flashes
And a rumbling filled the air
And then some splashes near us
And I wished I wasn't there
Now I was just enlisted
But I'd liked to know just where
The things I saw where happening
And were causing such a scare
I turned to an older shipmate
Who had been here once before
I figured he just had to know
Cause he always knew the score
He looked at me, then sniffed the air
And then stared straight ahead
A look of wisdom crossed his face
Fuck if I know's what he said

This is for all of us who didn't have the slightest ideas where we were,
<u>Most Of The Time</u>!

Wounds Of War

Some wounds of war

Are never seen

They're buried deep within

No open wound

No purple heart

No blemish on the skin

But these are wounds

That leave a scar

Upon our very soul

They tear our hearts

Cause misery

And take a heavy toll

Our bloodless wounds

Cause us to ask

Oh God, what was it for

We go through life

Not knowing why

We have these wounds of war

The Wife

She slept
Alone and lonely in her wedding bed
With dreams her man in her head

She dreamt
Of foreign places far away
And of the time he had to stay

She cried
Her man was not where he should be
Exposed to fire from the enemy

She woke
The dream she had, Had been too real
Her man was hit, And she could feel

She knew
Her man was gone, It filled her head
She was alone, Her man was dead

The Monument

It's just another monument
A monument made of stone
With perhaps some figures made of bronze
To represent flesh and bone

It's there just to remind us
Of the ones we lost, and where
To remember what they gave for us
And show them that we care

They did not want to give their lives
But did so just the same
They did not fight to rule the world
And they did not fight for fame

They fought and died for other men
In countries far away
And when they went, or where they went
In truth, they had no say

If all their names were listed now
As far as you could see
Remember them for what they did
They fought for liberty

Suits and Uniforms

There are some men who wear a suit
So they can look their best
But let me wear my uniform
With my ribbons on my chest
A suit will hide the real man
His life a mystery
But a man in a class "A" uniform
His history's there to see
His campaign ribbons tell the tale
Just where a man has been
The top row tells you what he's done
And the hell that he has seen
Never mind those fancy neckties
Those expensive silken suits
I would rather meet a real man
Still wearing combat boots

The Wind

The sighing, moaning wind, as lonely as a solitary, aging
Dying tree upon a bare granite mountain peak,
Fills my mind with nothingness

It's movement through my being disturbs the dust of
Memories long buried by my expertise at erasing so many
Things that caused such anguish at their occurrence

Or has the dust permeated my very soul, and has it been
There poisoning and eating at the marrow of my bones?

Has it been the cause of the torrents of tears shed by those
Closest to me?

Has it colored my nights with remembrances in brilliant
And screaming color, with all the sounds and smells of
Places, and things best forgotten?

The wind roars on and thoughts spiral upwards, some to
Float and catch the light of a setting sun, and others to
Settle again within the blackness and solitary emptiness of
My questioning mind

Whatever gods may be, please still the wind, and tell me

Why?

Death

I think of death and its rewards
Forever peace without a doubt
Or will it bring my strife renewed
Or is it the way out

I'm not allowed to seek my death
In that I have no voice
My God will take me That I know
In that I have no choice

My life has not been without sin
But not without regret
So many things were not the best
And I have evil met

Oh God, my God, Please hear my prayer
Please let me live in peace
Please take away the awful hurts
And let my troubles cease

Hillsides

The hillsides in their coats of green
Feed cattle waiting for the spring
Then colors bright as one has seen
A magic to those hills will bring

Deep purple and some yellow there
As angels have their earthly fling
With golden poppies everywhere
So bright it makes those angels sing

Yes, God's great treasures there to see
As famous paintings in a hall
God puts it there for you and me
For all of us, both great and small

Our hillsides wait throughout the year
For those short moments when they bloom
And when green grass shows spring is here
The hillsides color God's great room

The Wind of Faith

Oh God please help me find
The wind of faith within my soul
The wind of faith I need so much
Please let it play its role

I've searched and searched and haven't found
Through anguish, pain, and tears
And struggled with my conscience
These many many years

I've talked to you so many times
And I know that you are there
So that is not my problem
Cause I know you're everywhere

There's more to faith than words of praise
Acceptance is the key
To open up my heart and soul
And let you enter me

Oh God I'm here, a tortured soul
Please help me find some peace
Please help me find my way through life
Till all my troubles cease

Many Gifts, One Spirit

I have received so many gifts
So many in my life
I have received God's gift of faith
And God gave me my wife
My life is filled with wondrous gifts
It seems they'll never cease
His spirit is the greatest gift
A life of endless peace
Yes, troubles may arise at times
But troubles fade away
The spirit in me rises
When I pray to God each day

Winter

The air is getting crisper
The nights are growing long
And soon we will be feeling
The chill of winter's song
The wind will soon be howling
With notes which reach high C
And leaves will soon be falling
From every lonely tree
The sun will hide its friendly face
And clouds will fill the sky
Then way up in the mountains
The snow will start to fly
The earth is always ready
For this time of the year
It is the time for rest and peace
When winter's drawing near
Thanksgiving's the beginning
Then Christmas comes along
Replenishing our need for faith
To make our souls grow strong
The winter is a time for change
The sun will shine again
And winter brings the gift of life
Brought on by winter's rain
When winter weaves its magic
It readies all for spring
When flowers dot the mountainsides
And causes birds to sing

The Tiger

The razor clawed tiger
Of times past
Slips through my mind
So silently
Sometimes it springs
To pull me down
And bares its teeth
To gnaw at me

My tiger's wild
It has no soul
My tiger
Makes me grieve
And this I've learned
Throughout the years
My tiger'll
Never leave

Thoughts

Thoughts of past things
Hot as fire
Memories burning
On a bed of coals
A man twisting
On a funeral pyre
One of many
Of tormented souls
What have we done
To have this pain
The many things
We'll never tell
A placid life
We'll never gain
And when we die
We'll go to hell

Young Men

Young men old before their time
With hollow eyes and vacant stare
So many days of constant fear
So many friends no longer there

Those same young men now truly old
Their ranks grow thinner every day
They're getting ready to rejoin
The ones who died, who'll show the way

Some battles never seem to end
And others end with just a sigh
But these young men have seen it all
And face their fate, and never cry

Now others young will take their place
And learn to face another's death
To feel the thrill "I'm still alive"
And still feel sorrow with their breath

There'll always be young men grown old
The ones who faced our country's foe
With memories scarred forever more
Oh *God*, Oh *God*, must it be so

A Piece Of Metal

Somewhere a piece of metal is flying

Towards me

Its edges sharp and polished

Not yet stained with my blood

I have stayed away from death so long

That I feel free

But no matter how I twist and turn

It will do no good

Other pieces found my friends

And struck them down

They were so young, so very young

And now, they're gone

I'm still alive, but it follows me

From town to town

When will it strike, I'm so exposed

I'm so alone

Alone

There are people all around me
There are people everywhere
They are in the damnedest places
And where I go, they're there

But I'm alone

I move through them like a ghost
I speak, but they don't hear
I try to let them know, it's me
They don't even know I'm near

I'm all alone

Sometimes I meet another ghost
A traveler, just like me
But words are one thing we don't have
They're a long gone luxury

And we're alone

I wonder if I'll travel far
Before I find someone to tell
Or will I wander endlessly
Until I find my place in hell

And be alone

Buggin Out

What does the soul seek faraway
To just pass by and never stay
Does wandering ease the pain inside
The pain we strive so hard to hide
Why can't we sit to someone talk
To just stay there instead of walk
We never talk of those befores
We hide behind our shuttered doors
We dream our dreams of screaming sweat
Of all the ones we knew and met
The ones who met their final when
The ones who live when we think then
And once a year when we parade
To honor those who always stayed
We march with thousands of the hosts
Those friends of ours now only ghosts
And we can see them by our side
From us do they not have to hide
But from them comes familiar fear
And we fight back the running tear
And then the things we've hid so well
Come back to say we're back in hell
So then we look to find relief
Another place to ease our grief
A place we'll never ever find
Unless it's back with all our kind

When We Were Young

Remember all the fun we had
In times when things were bad
When we were young and full of life
And kept out all the sad
We'd spend all of our money
On young girls of the night
And the three words most important
Were *Women*, *Beer*, and *Fight*
Our yesterdays were far away
We left those far behind
We'd have to wait for later years
For our memories to unwind
Now was the time to raise some hell
Squeeze a lifetime in a day
Buy all the fun and joy we could
Before we went away
We all knew that it wouldn't last
But pretended t'wasn't so
That tomorrow we'd go back again
Back to the bad we'd go
It didn't seem like much back then
We were so young and bold
Those memories were the best we'd have
And the worst were never told.

From Boy To Man

I think of places
Dear to me
Those places where
I used to be
Those places where
I was a boy
And life to me
Was endless joy
But then I grew
Into a man
And did the things
That warriors can
I went to places
Cross the sea
Those places burning
In my memory
I'm home now
And I'm home to stay
But not the boy
Who went away
Somewhere I know
My soul was lost
My duties done
But at what cost

Ghostly Shadows

Their ghostly shadows wrapped in fear
Are with me sometimes oh so near
They're there I know but out of sight
They force me to sit down and write
Of things that happened to us all
For them I dream and I recall
And then I see them bright and clear
Their young fresh faces full of fear
And I wonder did they really know
When it was time for them to go
And I remember one young boy
Who should be living full of joy
Who asked me not to let him fight
He said he saw the coming night
But I said no, He had to go
And what he feared, Death made it so
Oh God, How many others are like me
So full of guilt and never free
With ghosts that wander through our head
Reminding us of youthful dead
So all my tears fall on the page
And hope that cools their silent rage

Heavy Darkness

The heavy darkness on my soul
So many years it took its toll
It seared it's blackness on my mind
The path of light I could not find
It was a maelstrom to the pit
And I was caught, Not fighting it
I'd cried for help from those ashore
My cries grew faint and then no more
I was now flotsam on the brine
There was no aid, There was no sign
I drifted slowly through my life
I'd given up, No fight nor strife
I could not continue on this course
The storm closed in with all it's force
To change my heading was my need
To sail towards light with all due speed
I now got help, We took the helm
And fought together to overwhelm
The storm was fierce and tore some sails
The seas were high and breached our rails
But we were winning, We passed the eye
The clouds swept by, We saw the sky
The sunlight came, Gone was the night
My course is set toward the light

I Wish I Knew Your Name

I knew you once upon a time
Like I knew many more
I think I knew your last name
Before I learned the score
You worked and slept alongside of me
A member of the crew
Not knowing you would soon be gone
Your life would soon be through
You did your duty on the gun
You were good at what you did
No one would think by watching you
That you were just a kid
I really don't know what it was
That hit you on that day
No time to stop, we carried on
No one knew what to say
Your place was filled by another kid
Who looked about the same
And now I wish I knew you then
I wish I knew your name

I'm Growing Old

The years go by, I'm growing old
Yet my memories are still new
The good ones and the bad ones
Of the bad ones, quite a few

I love the good ones, they are fun
They're bright just like the sun
The bad ones aren't fun at all
They make me want to run

I try to face them day to day
Just one day at a time
But when they wake me up at night
The walls I want to climb

I sweat and pant and try to shout
I sit straight up in bed
I wish those goddamn awful dreams
Would just vacate my head

I talk to friends I really know
To fix my thoughts in place
But the bad things will not go away
And the tears run down my face

I need to build my wall again
This time real high and strong
Just think of good things every day
And fill my life with song

Just Another Sailor

He was just another sailor
About ten thousand miles from home
Standing on a windswept pier
He was standing all alone
He had spent the day ashore
In a strange and foreign land
Just another port he'd been before
Another pier he'd have to stand
Waiting for the motor launch
That would take him back to sea
Aboard a U.S. Naval ship
Where he felt truly free
How many sailors like him
Have stood on windswept piers
Just waiting to go back to sea again
For all these many years

I'm So Happy

I'm so happy
I could just shit
All my damn stories
Are all a big hit
Outside I'm laughing
A big shit eating grin
No fucking worries
I'm sharp as a pin
My insides are bloody
They're torn all to hell
I just can't continue
What more can I tell
There's no one around me
Who knows how I feel
I just want some loving
I'm not made of steel
My pleas go unanswered
Like talking to stone
I may be surrounded
But I'm so fucking alone

Civilian

I've been a civilian for many a year
But I still remember the godawful fear
When the guns were all firing
Not all of them ours
And incoming airbursts
With the shrapnel so near

Cold as the devil but covered with sweat
The odds a real tossup with no one to bet
We all did our duty
We kept on firing the gun
I think those guys were the bravest
That I've ever met

All of us shouting to cover our fright
All of us hoping with all of our might
Don't let me be hurt
Don't let me be killed
Let me live through this battle
Let me live through this night

Now I'm a veteran, I paid my dues
Now all the fighting is all in the news
But some nights I wake up
Still hearing the guns
And remember the fear
That was felt by the crews

Grief

No matter the hurt, No matter the pain
You've got to ignore it, cause you're a man
Your insides are bleeding, your mind's torn to hell
But keep it all hidden, and laugh if you can

Don't let the grief get you, always keep your eyes dry
Just grit all those molars, and stick to the plan
Your guts maybe twisted from all you have seen
But remember your buddies, and that nobody ran

When death comes to claim you, it's then you can cry
Not now while your living, cause you are a man
Those were my lessons from the day I was born
So I grieve in my writing, cause I am a man

Caring

Sometimes I think about the past
And all the things I've done
Some really bad things that's for sure
And some things that were fun

Of all the guys I knew back then
And those who stayed behind
Whose names were all well known to me
And now they're from my mind

All the places that we went to
All the things we did back there
For all the things we did back then
We didn't seem to care

I saw some Chinese children
No grownups anywhere
No food or shelter for these kids
We didn't seem to care

So now I've grown much older
My memories are too much to bear
There's nothing I can do to change things
Now that I have grown to care

Of Birds And Men

A quail died in my hands today
It had flown into a window
And I felt its dying quiver
A lovely thing with a feather on its head
So beautiful and yet so dead
It brought my soul to shiver
There was no reason for its death
At least none that I could see
I just couldn't see the reason
Do the gods decide just what shall die
Do they set a certain time
Do they decide the season
I have seen men die just the same
A second of difference in their life
And they quivered in their dying
A pointless effort to save their life
For the gods made the decision
And I knew it was no use trying
But try we will and try we must
And every time we live on hope
Thinking that the gods are wrong
And I suppose we'll just keep on going
Till the last man leaves this earth
And the last bird sings it's song.

Golden Star

Oh Lord, why him, my flesh and blood
He was so young and strong
To take him in his youthful prime
Oh God, it seems so wrong
Why couldn't you wait a little while
To let him taste of life
To laugh and sing and be a man
To let him have a wife
I still remember when he left
So proud with head held high
He felt he could lift up the world
Nothing too hard to try
The telegram doesn't say much
But it broke my heart apart
With great regrets your son is gone
Cold words to soothe my heart
Through days and weeks and lonely years
I've missed my only son
Oh God why did you take away the light
Why did you hide the sun
My boy is gone, forever gone
Killed in a land so very far
And now I grieve, oh God I grieve
A Mom with a Golden Star

Another Way Of Asking

I have never been religious
And I've never learned to pray
But I've learned to write my poems
And to share what I can say
It is something deep within me
That makes me sit and write
As I fight to leave the darkness
And I grope towards the light
I guess prayer's what you make it
Standing tall or on your knees
It's another way of asking
One more way of saying "please?"
I'm not sure, and yet I'm certain
That there's someone watching me
Just to help me through the tough times
And to hear my every plea
So I'm hoping that there's someone
When there's a war, and when I ask
Please take care of all my buddies
Help them through their trying task
Do not let them feel the shrapnel
From the mines dug in the plain
Help them live to see the morning
Keep them safe and free from pain
All I ask is that you watch them
In those foreign lands they roam
But if they're hit and life is ebbing
Please welcome them into your home

The Deadly Garden

The desert blossoms

With the bright red blooms

Of fiery death

Large metal birds

Dart here and there

Searching

For the cores of living breath

The nectar of once living things

Flows red upon the sands of hell

The skies cloud up

And softly cry

Upon the many leaves that fell

Farewell

Farewell!
A word with meaning, oh so much
To leave the people you have known
To shake their hand with one last touch

Farewell!
How many times I've used that word
In many places far and wide
The very last that some friends heard

Farewell!
I've uttered last in many climes
And never knew if I'd return
I'll never know how many times

Farewell!
The word I've heard as boy and man
To watch my friends and buddies go
I sometimes cried, but never ran

Farewell!
It brings us joy or brings us pain
It's not forever just the same
Someday I'll see you all again

Farewell!

Healing

Once the rage and pain are gone
And the emptiness is all you have
You can start your life anew
Using time as healing salve

It's a time for healing scars
It's a time for pain to leave
Look forward to the future
And forget how much you grieve

All the cards that life may deal you
Are not always a winning hand
You can lose but keep on playing
Waiting for that ace to land

Life makes time to help the healing
Pushing all the hurt away
Erasing all the hurting memories
Helping all the good to stay

In time the healing does its wonders
Then we can laugh and show a smile
We look back, forget the bad things
Healing's working all the while

The Wrestling Match

The Pastor talked about Jacob
How he wrestled with God all night
How he only asked for God's blessing
After using all of his might

God then gave Jacob a new name
Israel is what he became
He was a taker before then
After that he was never the same

We are faced with all kinds of problems
And we think, God, how can this be
But God knows what he is doing
He's helping with adversity

Our bodies and souls need the challenge
We need to enter the fray
To accept the troubles which meet us
To wrestle with God every day

When the wind of life comes to bend us
We pray we'll always be strong
Our bodies and souls will be strengthened
With God's help we'll never go wrong

Now we face life's long lasting struggle
A struggle we must never lose
Because heaven awaits us forever
If Christ is the one who we choose

God's Magic

The magic of a brand new day
Sunshine bursting from the East
Mist rising from a winding stream
All bring to me my morning feast

Each day for me a wondrous gift
Which brings to me such inner peace
I look around, I'm filled with awe
Will God's great wonders never cease

My thank you to the sky I shout
I thank God for the life I love
The only question I may have
Is heaven here, or far above

Sunset

I watch the sun set
Far at sea
And wonder
When my time will be
So many reasons
Yet to live
So many years
I'd gladly give
Before the sunset
Comes the glow
Will that be me
Before I go
I have lived stormbound
Full of strife
While searching for
A peaceful life
I've seen the lightning
Burn the sky
And watched as others
Live and die
Someday will be
My time to go
When my sun sets
I hope I glow

A Prayer

I find myself so close to God
In waking and in sleep
I pray for health and longer life
For him my soul to keep

I dream about the songs I sing
My voice so loud and strong
My praises to the sky I fling
To Jesus I belong

The music fills my heart and soul
So beautiful the sound
The angels help me sing my song
They're with me all around

I'm just an ordinary man
Whose life is filled with love
For Jesus who has saved my life
And will welcome me above

I was a sinner, yes I was
But faith has brought me here
The place of promise waits for me
With my Lord always near

Oh God, Oh God, I'm just a man
My life to me is dear
Protect me from the ills of earth
And please, my Lord, stay near

Taps

Each box was covered with a flag

All lined up in a row

They looked so very elegant

In the early morning glow

The Skipper had some words to say

And the Chaplain spoke some too

The rest of us stood silently

As we honored those dead few

Then the haunting notes of *Taps* were heard

As sweet as a baby's sigh

A shudder ran through every man

As we said our last goodbye

Letter to a Veteran

So, you're a tough as nails Veteran, and you are not about to talk about a damn thing. I remember you! I put all the crap behind me, and besides who in hell wanted to listen what it was really like. John Wayne said it all. "We were a great bunch of guys", always won in the end, we were hardly scared at all, and felt great about the things we did and saw.

So we came home and took up our lives and did our best to be real genuine civilians. It kind of worked because most of us did o.k. We got jobs, went to school, got married, had families and tried to become normal. Hey! some of us actually made it. We did great. We became leaders of industry, got into politics, became active in church activities, led Boy Scouts and became respected members of our community.

Like it or not, some of us didn't. Even the ones who did might have problems that no one ever heard about. As a real tough Vet, you've probably never thought about the guys who didn't make it home.

Not once have you ever had a nightmare? Never had something happen that made you instinctively jump for cover? You've never been depressed as hell (let's not even mention thinking about ending it all)? All that stuff is for sissies and wimps, right? Yeah, you were me alright! And a lot of other guys, so don't feel like the Lone Ranger, you have a lot of company.

The great silent, don't talk about it (if you do you're a phony), it's all behind me, I'm never bothered—so called majority. You've never put your wife through hell, have you? You stuck to the first job you got for years, and felt real great about it? You never look for a seat with your back to the wall, and all the guns you own are strictly for hunting, right?

Yeah, you're right, us Vets don't talk about all of our experiences. We bury the stink, the unbelievable noise, the screams of old men, all of 18 or 19 years old. The total weariness we felt, and the fact we were all scared shitless a hell of a lot, right in our private little hell. If you are bothered, it's a lonely battle in your mind, not to be talked about. Damn, but are we tough or not?

Bullshit! We were stupid!

If enough of us had talked and told the truth, we might not have stopped a war from starting, but maybe just maybe, a lot of young, inexperienced, wide eyed recruits would have been a little more prepared. The training would have been better and the government more concerned about the guys actually doing the fighting, and the long lists of K.I.A. would have been shorter.

So you and I, and all the other guys who have seen the elephant, have a choice. We can keep on being tight lipped hard asses, or we can help ourselves and a lot of others by finally speaking out. There might be some things we might be a *little* ashamed of, but hey man, join the crowd. Things were not what you might call normal, and we probably weren't too normal either.

I know one thing for sure, after all those years of being a real tough bastard, I finally opened up and let some of it out. Damn, what a relief. I wasn't alone after all. There were a lot of others just like me out there. As bad as I felt at times, some of the guys were a whole lot worse off, and maybe now I could help and get help.

I just want you to know that you are just like all the rest of us. You might decide to leave well enough alone, but just once

try talking!

I highly recommend the following if you feel you need to talk to someone.

Vet Centers

http://www.va.gov/rcs/
1-800-905-4675 (Eastern)
1-800-496-8838 (Pacific)

978-0-595-46230-8
0-595-46230-8

Printed in the United States
122953LV00003B/223-231/A

9 780595 462308